Explore the Solar System

Jupiter
and the
Asteroids

WORLD
BOOK

a Scott Fetzer company
Chicago
www.worldbookonline.com

World Book, Inc.
233 N. Michigan Avenue
Chicago, IL 60601
U.S.A.

For information about other World Book publications, visit
our Web site at **http://www.worldbookonline.com** or call
1-800-WORLDBK (967-5325).

For information about sales to schools and
libraries, call **1-800-975-3250 (United States),**
or **1-800-837-5365 (Canada).**

Library of Congress Cataloging-in-Publication data
Jupiter and the asteroids.
   p. cm. -- (Explore the solar system)
   Summary: "An introduction to Jupiter and asteroids
for primary and intermediate grade students with
information about their features and exploration. Includes
a list of highlights for each chapter, fun facts, glossary,
resource list, and index" -- Provided by publisher.
   Includes index.
   ISBN 978-0-7166-9537-0
   1. Jupiter (Planet)--Juvenile literature. 2. Asteroids--
Juvenile literature. I. World Book, Inc.
   QB661.J857 2011
   523.45--dc22
                    2010014929

ISBN 978-0-7166-9533-2 (set)

Printed in China by Leo Paper Products, Ltd.,
   Heshan, Guangdong
1st printing August 2010

Staff
Executive Committee
Vice President and Chief Financial Officer:
   Donald D. Keller
Vice President and Editor in Chief: Paul A. Kobasa
Vice President, Licensing & Business Development:
   Richard Flower
Chief Technology Officer: Tim Hardy
Managing Director, International: Benjamin Hinton
Director, Human Resources: Bev Ecker

Editorial:
Associate Director, Supplementary Publications:
   Scott Thomas
Managing Editor, Supplementary Publications:
   Barbara A. Mayes
Senior Editor, Supplementary Publications:
   Kristina A. Vaicikonis
Manager, Research, Supplementary Publications:
   Cheryl Graham
Manager, Contracts & Compliance
(Rights & Permissions): Loranne K. Shields
Editor: Michael DuRoss
Writer: Dan Blunk
Indexer: David Pofelski

Graphics and Design:
Manager: Tom Evans
Coordinator, Design Development
   and Production: Brenda B. Tropinski
Contributing Photographs Editor: Carol Parden

Pre-Press and Manufacturing:
Director: Carma Fazio
Manufacturing Manager: Steven K. Hueppchen
Production/Technology Manager: Anne Fritzinger
Proofreader: Emilie Schrage

Picture Acknowledgments:
Cover front: NASA/JPL/University of Arizona; NASA/JPL-Caltech/T. Pyle (SSC);
WORLD BOOK illustration by Paul Perreault; Cover back: NASA/JPL-Caltech/UCLA.

Dagli Orti, The Art Archive 33; © Michael Carroll 29; Dreamstime 50, 56, 58; ESA 38;
© Calvin J. Hamilton 11; JPL 17, 26; NASA 15, 34; NASA/CalTech 23; NASA/ESA/UC,
Berkeley 9; NASA/JPL 18, 52, 53; NASA/Cornell University 30; NASA/Johns Hopkins
University Applied Physics Laboratory 54, 55; NASA/JPL/University of Arizona 36;
NASA/University of Arizona/LPL 24; NASA/University of Arizona/Southwest Research
Institute 18; NASA/Lunar and Planetary Institute 41; © Mark Garlick, Photo Researchers
44; © Detlev Ravenswaay, SPL/Photo Researchers 40; © SPL/Photo Researchers 49;
Shutterstock 12

Illustrations: WORLD BOOK illustration by Steve Karp 4, 42; WORLD BOOK illustration
by Paul Perreault 1, 7, 20, 47

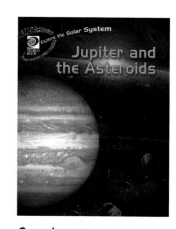

Cover image:
Jupiter orbits beyond a region
filled with millions of small rocky or
metallic objects called asteroids
(shown in a combined image).

Astronomers use different kinds of photos to learn about objects in space—such as
planets. Many photos show an object's natural color. Other photos use false colors.
Some false-color images show types of light the human eye cannot normally see.
Others have colors that were changed to highlight important features. When appro-
priate, the captions in this book state whether a photo uses natural or false color.

Contents

If a word is printed in **bold letters that look like this,** that word's meaning is given in the glossary on pages 60-61.

Where Is Jupiter?

Sun   Mercury Venus Earth Mars

Jupiter

Jupiter is the fifth **planet** from the sun in the **solar system.** Its **orbit** is, on average, about 484 million miles (779 million kilometers) from the sun.

Jupiter is the innermost of what **astronomers** call the outer planets. The other outer planets are Saturn, Uranus (*YUR uh nuhs* or *yu RAY nuhs*), and Neptune.

Jupiter's orbit is between the orbits of the planets Mars and Saturn. Mars is Jupiter's closest neighbor.

Uranus   **Neptune**

Saturn

Jupiter is about five times as far from the sun as Earth is. At their closest distance, the two planets are about 366 million miles (589 million kilometers) apart. If a jet airplane could fly through space—at 500 miles (800 kilometers) per hour—it would take about 84 years for it to reach Jupiter.

Highlights

- Jupiter is the fifth planet from the sun in the solar system.
- It is about 484 million miles (779 million kilometers) from the sun.
- Jupiter is the innermost of the four outer planets.
- Its orbit lies between those of Mars and Saturn.

How Big Is Jupiter?

Jupiter is massive. In fact, Jupiter is the largest **planet** in the **solar system**. Jupiter's **diameter** at its **equator** is about 88,846 miles (142,984 kilometers). That is about 11 times the diameter of Earth. Jupiter takes up so much space that if it were hollow, more than 1,300 Earths would fit inside.

Jupiter is not only the largest planet in the solar system, but also has the most **mass.** Mass is the amount of matter, or material, a thing contains. Jupiter has more mass than all of the other planets of the solar system combined.

Jupiter lies at the center of a vast system of cosmic objects. Dozens of **satellites** and four faint rings of dust particles **orbit** the planet. Astronomers sometimes refer to the planet and its satellites and rings as the Jovian system.

Highlights

- Jupiter is the largest planet in the solar system.
- It is also the most massive, having more mass than all the other planets put together.
- Jupiter's diameter at its equator is 88,846 miles (142,984 kilometers).
- Jupiter and its rings and satellites are sometimes known as the Jovian system.

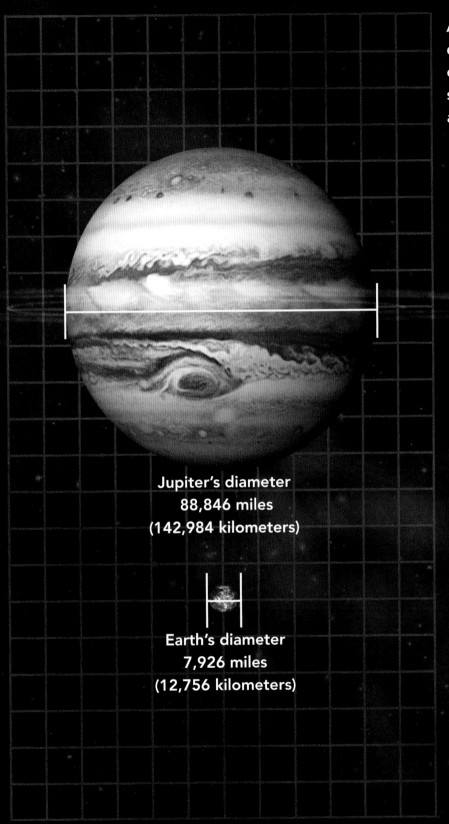

An artist's drawing comparing the size of Jupiter and Earth

Jupiter's diameter
88,846 miles
(142,984 kilometers)

Earth's diameter
7,926 miles
(12,756 kilometers)

What Does Jupiter Look Like?

From Earth, Jupiter is one of the brightest objects in the night sky. The only objects that are usually brighter than Jupiter are Earth's **moon** and the **planet** Venus. Jupiter's most visible features are bands of light clouds and belts of dark clouds. They range from orange-brown to bluish white.

Jupiter's **atmosphere** also has many oval or circular features. A gigantic, reddish, oval object that is larger than Earth is visible on the southern half of the planet. Scientists call this feature the Great Red Spot. They think the Great Red Spot is a huge storm that has existed for hundreds of years. In the late 1990's and early 2000's, three white ovals combined to form a larger oval that turned reddish. The new spot is often called the Little Red Spot.

Highlights

- Jupiter is one of the brightest objects in the night sky and can be seen from Earth without a telescope or binoculars.

- It is covered with clouds of gas that form bands of colors ranging from orange-brown to bluish white.

- One of Jupiter's most well-known features is called the Great Red Spot.

Great Red Spot

Little Red Spot

Jupiter's bright bands and belts appear in a natural-color photograph made with the Hubble Space Telescope.

What Is Jupiter Made Of?

Scientists call **planets** like Jupiter **gas giants** because they are made up mostly of gas and do not have a solid surface. Jupiter consists mainly of the gas **hydrogen.** It also contains small amounts of **helium** and other heavier chemical **elements.** Most of the elements in Jupiter's **atmosphere** consist of **atoms** that are are combined into molecules of water, ammonia, and other substances.

Jupiter's outer layer is made chiefly of hydrogen gas. Below that is a layer of liquid hydrogen. The powerful pressure of the gas layer above has caused hydrogen atoms there to squeeze together and become a liquid. About 6,000 miles (10,000 kilometers) below the clouds, the pressure causes the liquid hydrogen to turn into liquid metallic hydrogen. This unusual form of hydrogen conducts electricity like a regular metal.

Highlights

- Astronomers call Jupiter a gas giant.
- The planet consists mainly of hydrogen gas, with a small amount of helium gas and other substances.
- Inside Jupiter is a rocky core surrounded by layers of liquid metallic hydrogen, liquid hydrogen, and hydrogen gas.

Inside Jupiter

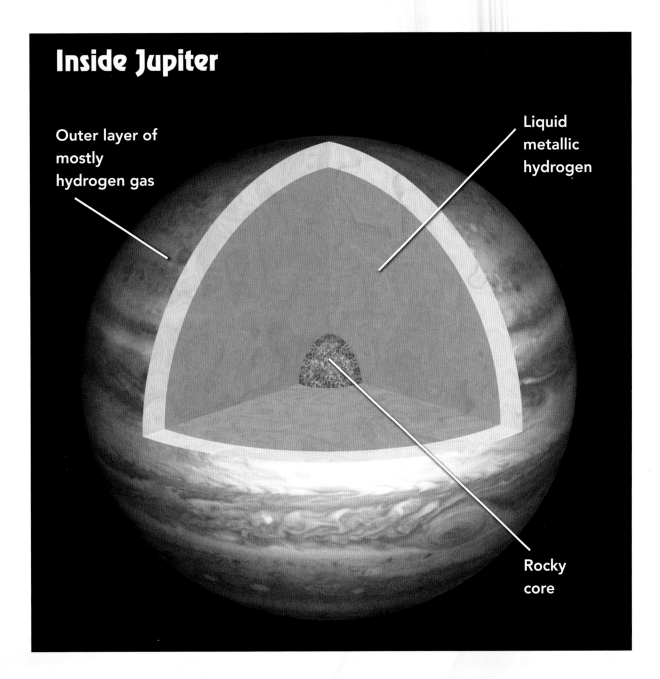

Outer layer of mostly hydrogen gas

Liquid metallic hydrogen

Rocky core

Scientists think that below the liquid metallic hydrogen Jupiter may have a dense **core** made up of heavier substances normally found in rock. This core may have 10 to 15 times as much **mass** as the entire planet Earth.

How Does Jupiter Compare with Earth?

Jupiter has hundreds of times the **mass** of Earth. But Jupiter's average **density** is much lower than Earth's. (Density is the amount of matter in a given space.) In fact, Jupiter is only a bit more dense than liquid water on Earth. Jupiter's density is so low because it is made mostly of the lightest **elements—hydrogen** and **helium** gases. Earth is a rocky planet made of mostly heavier materials.

Because Jupiter has much more mass than Earth, its **gravity** is much stronger. Jupiter's gravity is about 2 ½ times as strong as that of Earth. If you weighed 100 pounds (45 kilograms) on Earth, you would weigh about 240 pounds on Jupiter, the equivalent of 109 kilograms on Earth.

Highlights

- Jupiter is hundreds of times as massive as Earth.
- Earth is more dense than Jupiter because Jupiter is made mostly of gases and light elements.
- Because Jupiter has more mass than Earth, its gravity is much stronger than Earth's.

How Do They Compare?

	Earth	Jupiter
Size in diameter (at equator)	7,926 miles (12,756 kilometers)	88,846 miles (142,984 kilometers)
Average distance from sun	About 93 million miles (150 million kilometers)	About 484 million miles (779 million kilometers)
Length of year (in Earth days)	365.25	4,332.5
Length of day (in Earth time)	24 hours	9 hours 56 minutes
What an object would weigh...	If it weighed 100 pounds (45 kilometers) on Earth...	...it would weigh about 240 pounds (the equiva-, lent of 109 kilograms) on Jupiter.
Number of moons	1	16 large moons, about 50 smaller moons
Rings	No	Yes
Atmosphere	Nitrogen, oxygen, and small amounts of argon, water vapor, and carbon dioxide	Hydrogen, helium, methane, ammonia, carbon monoxide, ethane, acetylene, phosphine, and water vapor

What Is Jupiter's Atmosphere Made Of?

Jupiter's **atmosphere** is made up mostly of **hydrogen** and **helium** gases. Clouds in the lower atmosphere give the **planet** its colorful, banded appearance. The clouds that are most visible from space are made up mainly of icy particles of **ammonia** (*uh MOHN yuh* or *uh MOH nee uh*).

Highlights

- Most of Jupiter's atmosphere is made up of hydrogen and helium gas.
- The clouds in Jupiter's lower atmosphere form the colored bands that we see.
- The clouds are made of color-less ammonia ice; tiny amounts of other chemicals give them their colors.

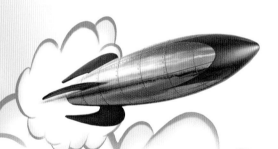

Fun Fact

The largest storm in Jupiter's atmosphere—called the Great Red Spot—is wider than the diameter of Earth!

By themselves, ammonia clouds are colorless. Jupiter's clouds are colorful because they contain small amounts of other chemicals. Slight differences in the *altitude* (height) of these clouds cause differences in the brightness of the bands. Bands at high altitudes reflect more sunlight. So they appear brighter than clouds at lower altitudes.

Scientists think there may be other types of clouds beneath the ammonia clouds. A second layer may have clouds made of a substance that contains hydrogen, nitrogen, and sulfur. Below that may be a cloud layer of **water ice** (frozen water).

Bands of clouds on Jupiter in a natural-color photo

What Is the Weather Like on Jupiter?

The weather on Jupiter is very cloudy and windy. The winds on Jupiter blow very hard and can reach speeds of about 400 miles (650 kilometers) per hour near the **equator.**

Storms on Jupiter can last a long time. The Great Red Spot, the largest of the **planet's** storms, has been visible from Earth since at least 1831. The Great Red Spot is slowly shrinking. But it is still so big that the entire Earth could fit inside.

Lightning bolts more powerful than any on Earth flash in Jupiter's **atmosphere. Astronomers** first observed lightning on Jupiter in images from the Voyager space **probe.** They later determined that the lightning comes from small cloud plumes that resemble thunderheads on Earth.

Highlights

- Jupiter's weather is cloudy and windy, with storms that last for a long time.
- The most famous storm on Jupiter is the Great Red Spot.
- Temperatures on Jupiter vary widely, with the hottest temperatures in the core and the coolest at the cloud tops.

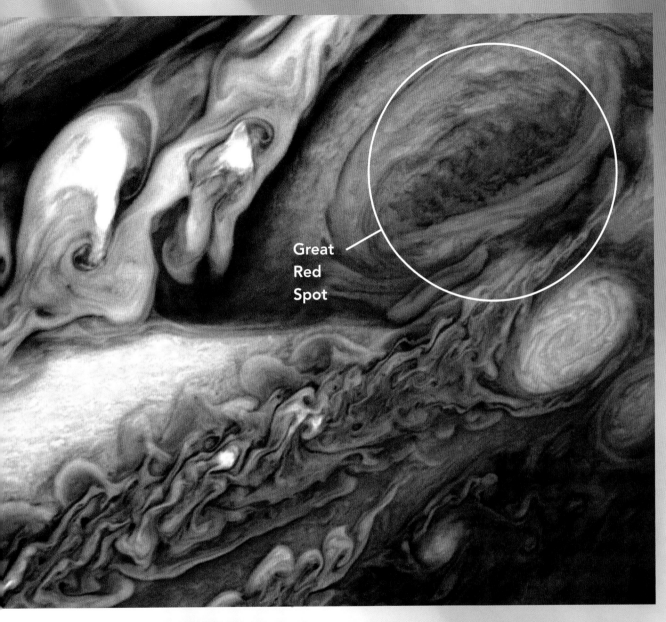

Great Red Spot

Temperatures on Jupiter vary widely by *altitude* (height) and location. Near Jupiter's cloud tops, the temperature is roughly -236 °F (-149 °C). In contrast, the **core** of the planet may be up to 43,000 °F (24,000 °C)—hotter than the surface of the sun.

Swirling clouds in the Great Red Spot have been darkened in a false-color photograph to reveal detail.

How Fast Do Winds Blow on Jupiter?

The winds on Jupiter are very powerful. The **planet's** winds blow the fastest along the **equator.** There they can reach speeds of up to 400 miles (650 kilometers) per hour, almost twice as fast as the most devastating hurricane winds on Earth.

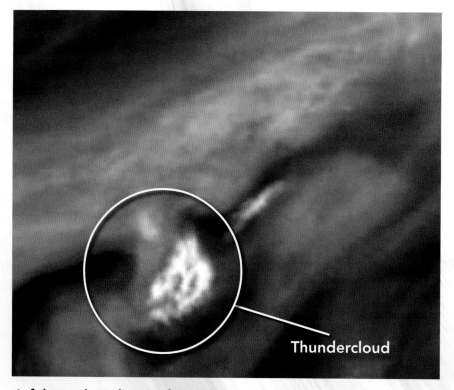

Thundercloud

A false-color photo of Jupiter's atmosphere includes a white area that represents a thundercloud. The upper level of the cloud was made of ammonia ice.

False-color images taken by NASA's New Horizons spacecraft track an ammonia cloud as it forms over two days on Jupiter. At first, the cloud is barely visible as a short, light blue stripe (below) and enlarged (right, top). Ten hours later, as the gas warms and rises, the cloud becomes brighter and longer (right, middle). Twenty hours later, the cloud has spread out as it cools and begins to sink (right, bottom).

Ammonia cloud

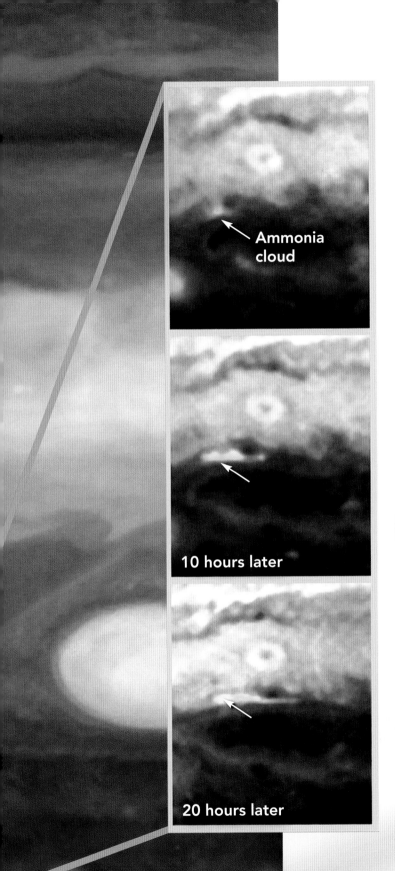

Ammonia
cloud

10 hours later

20 hours later

Scientists think **convection currents** (circulation patterns based on temperatures) power Jupiter's winds. This process on Jupiter can be seen from space. The pale bands of clouds on Jupiter are actually areas where the temperature is warmer and the clouds and gases are rising. The darker bands are cooler areas where the clouds and gases are sinking.

Highlights

- Very fast winds blow on Jupiter.
- The fastest winds are at the equator.
- Jupiter's winds may reach speeds of up to 400 miles (650 kilometers) per hour.
- The winds are powered by a process in which warm gases rise and cooler gases sink.

How Does Jupiter Move Around the Sun?

Jupiter takes a long time to complete one **orbit** around the sun. Jupiter is about 484 million miles (779 million kilometers) from the sun. The **planet** is more than five times farther from the sun than Earth is. Because it is so far away, Jupiter takes almost 12 Earth years to make a complete orbit. That is the length of a **year** on Jupiter.

Fun Fact

The metallic hydrogen around Jupiter's core gives the planet the strongest magnetic field in the solar system. This magnetic field creates a dangerous radiation belt around Jupiter that can damage visiting spacecraft.

Highlights

- It takes Jupiter about 12 Earth years to complete one orbit around the sun; so one year on Jupiter is nearly 12 Earth years long.
- But Jupiter spins on its axis faster than any other planet; one day on Jupiter is less than 10 hours long.

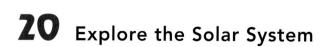

The Orbit and Rotation of Jupiter

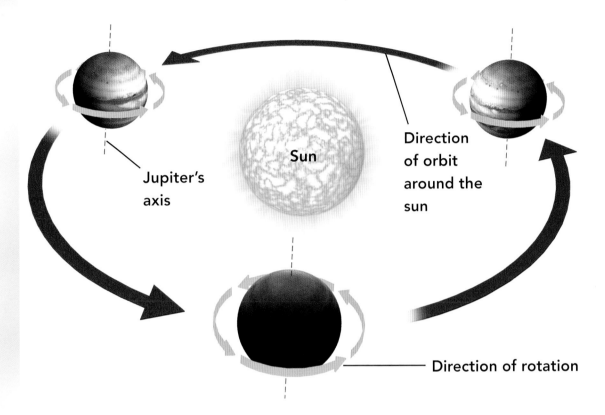

Jupiter's axis

Sun

Direction of orbit around the sun

Direction of rotation

Despite its size, Jupiter *rotates* (spins around) faster on its axis than any other planet in the **solar system.** (The axis is an imaginary line that passes through the planet.) As a result, Jupiter has the shortest **day.** Earth makes a complete rotation about every 24 hours. Jupiter's day lasts slightly less than 10 hours.

Because Jupiter rotates so quickly, the planet's shape is not perfectly round. Instead, Jupiter bulges slightly along the **equator.**

Does Jupiter Have a Surface?

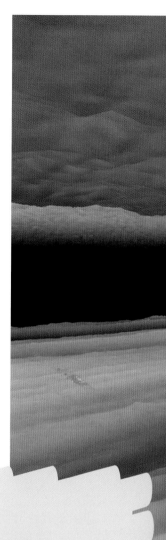

To an observer from space, Jupiter's cloud tops may look like a solid surface. But no one could stand on the surface of Jupiter. Although Jupiter has a very thick **atmosphere,** the clouds and gases are not thick enough to support people standing on top of them.

If Jupiter did have a surface, that surface would be very cold and windy. Jupiter is five times as far from the sun as Earth and so does not receive nearly as much heat from the sun as Earth does. However, Jupiter *radiates* (gives off) nearly twice as much heat as it absorbs from the sun. Scientists believe that some of this heat is energy left over from Jupiter's formation as a **planet.** Some of the energy might come from heat created as Jupiter slowly shrinks under the influence of **gravity.**

Highlights

- Jupiter has no solid surface.
- It has a thick atmosphere that is very cold and windy.
- Jupiter gives off about twice as much heat as it absorbs from the sun.
- The winds and storms occur as hot temperatures inside Jupiter cause gases to rise, cool, and fall again.

The high temperatures deep within Jupiter cause the gases in its lower atmosphere to heat up and rise. These gases gradually cool as they move upward. The movement of the gases causes very strong winds and windstorms.

Jupiter's clouds look almost like a solid surface in a 3-dimensional (3-D), false-color photograph.

How Many Moons Does Jupiter Have?

Astronomers have discovered more **moons** around Jupiter than around any other **planet** in the **solar system.** Jupiter's moons vary widely in size, color, **atmosphere,** and **density.**

Jupiter has 16 moons that are at least 6 miles (10 kilometers) in **diameter.** In addition, Jupiter has dozens of smaller moons—about 50 at last count! Scientists think some of Jupiter's smaller moons have yet to be discovered. Because so many moons, rings, and other objects orbit Jupiter, astronomers sometimes describe Jupiter and its moons as a mini-solar system.

Fun Fact

Three of Jupiter's moons—Io, Ganymede, and Callisto—are all bigger than Earth's moon.

Highlights

- Jupiter has 16 moons that are at least 6 miles (10 kilometers) across and dozens of smaller moons, some of which have not yet been discovered.

- Jupiter's moons are very different from one another in color, density, size, and atmosphere.

One of Jupiter's larger moons, Io, in a false-color photo made from several combined images

What Are the "Galilean Moons"?

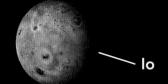

Io

Four of Jupiter's **moons** are so large that they are visible from Earth to observers using a simple telescope. The Italian **astronomer** Galileo (*gal uh LAY oh* or *gal uh LEE oh*) discovered these moons in 1610. They are sometimes called the Galilean moons in his honor. The discovery of moons orbiting another planet helped convince Galileo and others that Earth was not at the center of the universe.

Europa

Ganymede

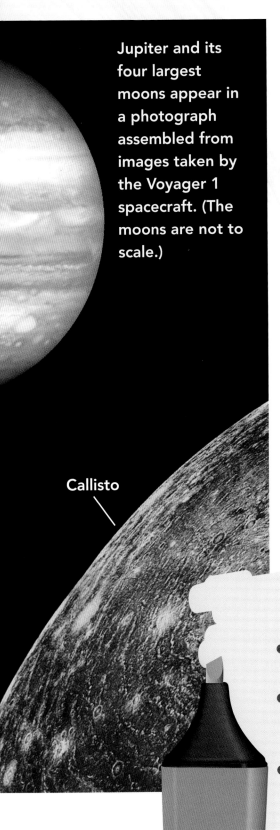

Jupiter and its four largest moons appear in a photograph assembled from images taken by the Voyager 1 spacecraft. (The moons are not to scale.)

Callisto

Io *(YE oh)* is the closest of the Galilean moons to Jupiter. It has more volcanic activity than any other body in the **solar system,** including Earth.

Europa *(yu ROH puh)* has many cracks, valleys, ridges, pits, and blisters on its surface. Many scientists think that beneath the moon's icy crust are deep oceans of liquid water or slushy **water ice.**

Ganymede *(GAN uh meed)* is the largest of Jupiter's moons. It is also the largest moon in the solar system—larger than Earth's moon and even the planet Mercury.

Callisto *(kuh LIHS toh)* is the farthest Galilean moon from Jupiter. It is almost completely covered in **craters.**

Highlights

- Italian astronomer Galileo discovered Jupiter's four largest moons.
- These moons—named Io, Europa, Ganymede, and Callisto—are also called the Galilean moons.
- Io is the closest moon to Jupiter and Callisto is the farthest. Ganymede is the largest.

What Are Some of Jupiter's Other Moons?

Jupiter has many other moons in addition to the Galilean **moons.** Scientists have divided these moons into two groups: the inner **satellites** and the outer satellites. The inner satellites are closer to Jupiter than the Galilean moons. The outer satellites are farther away.

Highlights

- Besides the Galilean moons, other moons of Jupiter have been placed into two groups called the inner satellites and the outer satellites.
- The inner satellites—named Metis, Adrastea, Amalthea, and Thebe—are closer to Jupiter than the Galilean moons.
- The outer satellites are farther from Jupiter than the Galilean moons.

Most of Jupiter's moons are named after figures in Greek and Roman mythology. Here are the names of Jupiter's four inner moons:

- Metis (*MEE this*), named after the Greek goddess of wisdom.
- Adrastea (*uh DRAS tee uh*), named after the Roman nymph who distributed rewards and punishments.
- Amalthea (*am uhl THEE uh*), named after a nymph who nursed the Greek god Zeus in his youth. Zeus is the Greek ruler of the gods. Jupiter is the Roman version of Zeus.
- Thebe (*THEE bee*), named after a daughter of Zeus.

Astronomers continue to discover additional moons **orbiting** Jupiter. Some of these moons are extremely small, less than 1.2 miles (2 kilometers) in **diameter.**

Amalthea, one of the inner satellites, is dwarfed by Jupiter in an artist's drawing.

Jupiter and the Asteroids 29

Does Jupiter Have Rings?

Astronomers were not sure that Jupiter had rings until 1979. That year, two space **probes** called Voyager 1 and Voyager 2 flew by Jupiter. The probes had been launched by the United States National Aeronautics and Space Administration (NASA) in 1977 to explore the outer **planets** and beyond. During their **fly-bys,** the Voyager probes took pictures of what appeared to be at least two rings.

Additional pictures taken with NASA's Galileo probe during the 1990's revealed that Jupiter has four rings. The brightest is called the main ring. A fainter ring is called the halo ring, and two even fainter rings are called the gossamer rings. Jupiter's rings are much fainter than the rings around Saturn.

Highlights

- Astronomers learned that Jupiter has rings when the U.S. space probes Voyager 1 and Voyager 2 took pictures of them in 1979.
- All four of Jupiter's rings are fainter than Saturn's rings.
- Astronomers think the rings formed when meteoroids knocked tiny bits of dust loose from Jupiter's inner satellites.

Gossamer rings

Main ring

Halo ring

Adrastea

Metis

Amalthea

Thebe

Astronomers think that the rings are made of extremely tiny *particles* (pieces) of dust. The particles appear to have been knocked from Jupiter's inner moons by collisions with small **meteoroids.** The edges of the rings correspond to the orbits of the four inner satellites.

A diagram of Jupiter's four rings and the four inner satellites

Jupiter and the Asteroids

How Did Jupiter Get Its Name?

Ancient **astronomers** knew about Jupiter because the **planet** can easily be seen with the unaided eye. These astronomers may not have known exactly what Jupiter was, but they tracked it as it moved across the night sky.

Because the planet was so large and bright, the ancient Romans named it after Jupiter, their most powerful god. Jupiter was the god of the sky and of thunder and lightning in Roman mythology. He used a

Highlights

- Ancient astronomers knew about Jupiter because it was so large and bright, they could see it in the night sky.
- The ancient Romans named the planet after their most powerful god.

A relief sculpture of the Roman god Jupiter

thunderbolt as a weapon. The Romans believed Jupiter had the power to send Earth clear weather, rain, or destructive storms. Jupiter was also worshiped as the ruler of the gods and of the universe. Jupiter is the Roman equivalent of the Greek god Zeus.

Which Space Missions Have Studied Jupiter?

NASA's Galileo probe approaches Io (left) and Jupiter, in an artist's drawing.

Many space missions have studied Jupiter. In 1973, the NASA **probe** Pioneer 10 became the first spacecraft to fly past Jupiter. In 1974, Pioneer 11 (later re-named Pioneer-Saturn) studied Jupiter. Both probes sent back information about Jupiter's **atmosphere, gravity,** and **magnetic field.**

In 1979, the NASA probes Voyager 1 and Voyager 2 made **fly-bys** of Jupiter. These probes studied Jupiter's atmosphere, discovered its rings, and photo-graphed many of its **moons.**

NASA's Ulysses probe, whose main purpose was to study the sun, swung past Jupiter in 1992. The probe studied radio signals sent out by the **planet** as well as dust and other particles **orbiting** the planet. Ulysses flew past again in 2003 and 2004 to study Jupiter's magnetic field.

Probably the most important mission to Jupiter was NASA's Galileo probe. Galileo reached Jupiter in 1995 and became the first probe to orbit the planet. Galileo released a small probe that became the first instrument to sample the atmosphere of a **gas giant.**

NASA's Cassini spacecraft observed Jupiter on its way to Saturn in 2000. In 2007, the New Horizons spacecraft took photos of a storm on Jupiter called the Little Red Spot while traveling toward Pluto.

Highlights

- Many space missions have studied Jupiter since the first probe, Pioneer 10, flew past the planet in 1973.
- The NASA probes Voyager 1, Voyager 2, and Galileo dis-covered much of what we know about Jupiter's atmosphere, its rings, and its moons.

Could There Be Life on Jupiter or Its Moons?

Jupiter has no real surface because it is made mostly of gas. In addition, the **planet** has extreme temperatures and no bodies of water. Its force of **gravity** is also much stronger than Earth's. Scientists do not think life as we know it could exist on Jupiter.

But some of Jupiter's **moons** may have the conditions needed for life. Many scientists think that Europa may have an ocean of liquid water beneath its frozen surface. And, where there is water, there could be living organisms.

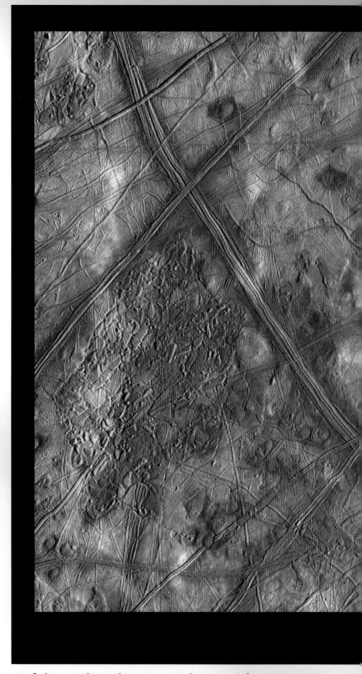

A false-color close-up (above) of part of Jupiter's moon Europa (right) shows blue areas that scientists think are icy plains.

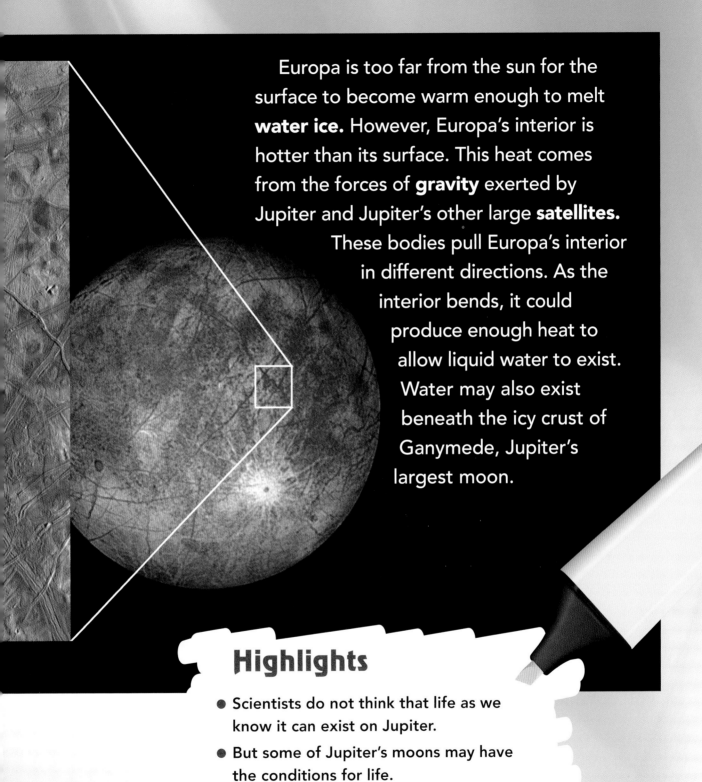

Europa is too far from the sun for the surface to become warm enough to melt **water ice.** However, Europa's interior is hotter than its surface. This heat comes from the forces of **gravity** exerted by Jupiter and Jupiter's other large **satellites.** These bodies pull Europa's interior in different directions. As the interior bends, it could produce enough heat to allow liquid water to exist. Water may also exist beneath the icy crust of Ganymede, Jupiter's largest moon.

Highlights

- Scientists do not think that life as we know it can exist on Jupiter.
- But some of Jupiter's moons may have the conditions for life.
- Both Europa and Ganymede may have liquid water beneath their icy surfaces.

What Are Jupiter's Rocky Neighbors?

Jupiter's rocky neighbors are **asteroids.** Asteroids are irregularly shaped objects that were left over from the formation of the **solar system** billions of years ago. Scientists estimate that there are millions of asteroids.

Most asteroids are made of metals or rocky material or are rich in **minerals** containing carbon. Like **planets,** asteroids rotate as they **orbit** the sun. But asteroids are too small to be planets. The largest asteroid, Ceres, is classified as a dwarf planet.

Asteroids can range in size from about 600 miles (965 kilometers) in **diameter** to less than 20 feet (6 meters) across. Some asteroids are large enough to have their own **moon.** For example, the asteroid Ida has a small moon named Dactyl.

Highlights

- Jupiter orbits near an area that contains millions of irregularly shaped objects called asteroids.
- Scientists believe asteroids are left over from the formation of the solar system billions of years ago.
- Asteroids can be as small as 20 feet (6 meters) across or as large as 600 miles (965 kilometers) across.

The European Space Agency's Rosetta spacecraft, launched in 2004, passes an asteroid on its way to a comet, in an artist's drawing.

What Is the Main Belt?

Main Belt

Most of the **asteroids** in the **solar system** are found in one area—between the **orbits** of the **planets** Jupiter and Mars. This region is known as the asteroid belt, or the **Main Belt.**

Scientists have discovered that the Main Belt has two parts with different types of asteroids in each area. The outer part of the Main Belt contains asteroids that are rich in carbon—a chemical

- Most asteroids are found in the Main Belt, an area between the orbits of Jupiter and Mars.
- Carbon-rich asteroids are in the outer part of the Main Belt; mineral-rich asteroids are in the inner part.
- Trojan asteroids orbit outside the Main Belt, near Jupiter.

The Main Belt, shown in an artist's illustration (left), lies between the orbits of Mars and Jupiter.

element. These asteroids are very old and have not changed much since the solar system formed 4.6 billion years ago.

The asteroids in the inner part of the Main Belt, which is closer to Earth, contain many metal-rich **minerals.** Scientists think these asteroids formed at very high temperatures.

Located outside the Main Belt are two groups of asteroids called Trojan asteroids. These asteroids circle just ahead and just behind Jupiter in its orbit. They are named for heroes of the Trojan War in Greek legend.

Are All Asteroids Found in the Main Belt?

Although the vast majority of **asteroids** are near Jupiter in the **Main Belt,** or asteroid belt, some are **orbiting** in other areas of the **solar system.** Many of these asteroids are known as near-Earth asteroids. Near-Earth asteroids are grouped according to their orbits. They are called Atens, Apollos, or Amors.

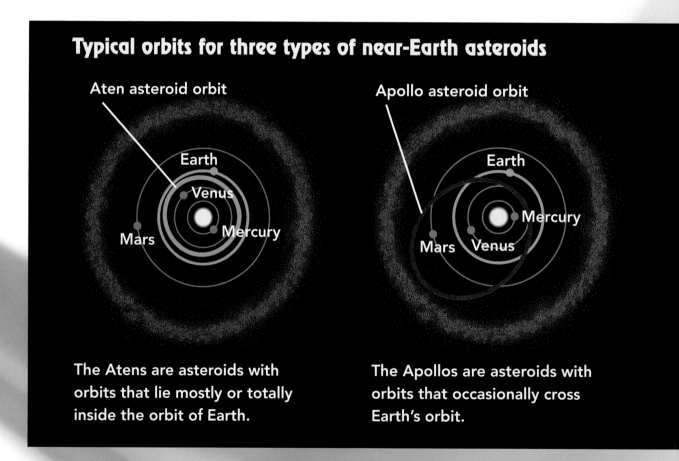

Typical orbits for three types of near-Earth asteroids

Aten asteroid orbit

Apollo asteroid orbit

The Atens are asteroids with orbits that lie mostly or totally inside the orbit of Earth.

The Apollos are asteroids with orbits that occasionally cross Earth's orbit.

Highlights

- Besides the Main Belt asteroids, there are also near-Earth asteroids, Trojans, and Centaurs.
- Near-Earth asteroids are found between the orbits of Earth and Mars. Trojans follow the same orbit as Jupiter. Centaurs are outside the solar system and may actually be comets.

Each of these types of asteroids is named for a single asteroid that it resembles. That is, the Atens are named for a specific asteroid named Aten.

There are also asteroids called Trojans (see the diagram on page 41) that follow the same orbit as Jupiter. And there are a few asteroids in the outer areas of the solar system. These are called Centaurs, and at least some of them could be **comets** instead of asteroids.

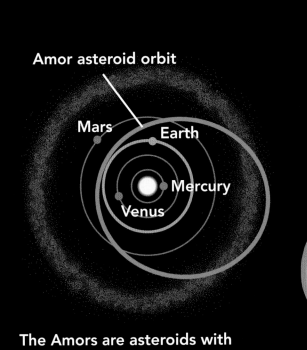

Amor asteroid orbit

Mars

Earth

Mercury

Venus

The Amors are asteroids with orbits that cross the orbit of Mars but not of Earth.

Fun Fact

Even though scientists estimate that there are millions of asteroids, the average distance between those in the Main Belt is about 62,000 miles (100,000 kilometers).

What Is Ceres?

Ceres (*SIHR eez*) was the first **asteroid** ever discovered. Scientists know from telescope observations that Ceres has a relatively smooth, dark surface that consists of clay-like **minerals** that contain **water ice.**

Ceres is the largest asteroid in the **Main Belt.** Its **mass** is equal to one-fourth of the mass of all the other asteroids in the Main Belt combined. At its longest, Ceres has a **diameter** of 596 miles (960 kilometers). At its shortest, it is 579 miles (932 kilometers) wide. Ceres is less than one-third the size of Earth's **moon.**

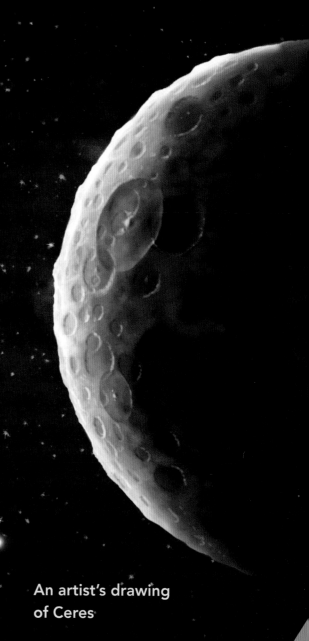

An artist's drawing of Ceres

A photo of Ceres taken with the Hubble Space Telescope

Highlights

- Ceres is the largest asteroid in the Main Belt.
- Ceres is also considered a dwarf planet.
- Ceres is a little less than one-third the size of Earth's moon.
- Ceres probably formed from the collisions of many smaller objects early in the history of the solar system.

In 2006, some **astronomers** began to classify Ceres as both an asteroid and a **dwarf planet.** The International Astronomical Union (IAU), a widely recognized authority in naming heavenly bodies, adopted a standard definition for the term *planet.* The group also created a category called dwarf planets. Like planets, dwarf planets orbit the sun and are round. But dwarf planets do not have enough gravitational pull to sweep the region of their orbit relatively free of other objects.

Ceres probably formed early in the history of the **solar system** from many smaller bodies that collided and stuck together. But scientists think the force of **gravity** from nearby Jupiter prevented additional bodies from attaching to Ceres. So Ceres never grew to the size of a planet.

Where Is Ceres?

Ceres is in the **Main Belt,** between the orbits of Mars and Jupiter. That puts Ceres at the outer edge of the inner **planets** (Mercury, Venus, Earth, and Mars). Ceres is, on average, about 257 million miles (414 million kilometers) from the sun. The **orbit** of Ceres is closer to that of Mars than to Jupiter.

In 2007, NASA launched a space **probe** named Dawn on a mission to Ceres and Vesta, the third largest **asteroid** in the Main Belt. Dawn was to visit Vesta first. Telescope observations have revealed that the surface of Vesta consists mainly of basalt, a hard, dark volcanic rock. Scientists have identified **meteorites** found on Earth that probably came from Vesta. Dawn was to spend a year studying Vesta then fly on to Ceres. Dawn was expected to reach Ceres in 2015.

Both Ceres and Vesta formed about 4.5 billion years ago, early in the history of the **solar system.** By studying these primitive bodies, scientists hope to learn more about conditions in the early solar system and how planets form.

Highlights

- Ceres lies in the Main Belt, between Mars and Jupiter.
- Ceres is closer to Mars than to Jupiter.
- Scientists hope to learn more about Ceres when a NASA mission called Dawn, launched in 2007, reaches the asteroid.

Jupiter

Ceres

Asteroid belt

Mars

An artist's drawing
showing the location
of Ceres

Jupiter and the Asteroids **47**

Who Discovered Ceres?

An Italian **astronomer,** a monk named Giuseppe Piazzi (*joo ZEHP peh PYAHT tsee*), first spotted Ceres in 1801. He named the object for the Roman goddess of grain and the harvest. Piazzi tracked Ceres for several weeks but then lost track of the object in the sun's glare. In fall 1801, the German mathematician Carl Friedrich Gauss (*FREE drihk GOWS*) predicted the place in the sky where astronomers should look to find Ceres again. Within several months, a German astronomer named Heinrich Wilhelm Olbers located Ceres.

At first, some scientists thought Ceres was a "missing **planet**" thought to be orbiting between the **orbits** of Mars and Jupiter. In 1802, the British astronomer William Herschel (*HUR shuhl*) introduced the word **asteroid** to apply to Ceres and another object found in that year, named Pallas. (The word *asteroid* comes from a Greek word meaning *star-like*.)

Highlights

- An Italian astronomer named Giuseppe Piazzi discovered Ceres in 1801.
- Most astronomers at that time considered Ceres and other objects like it to be planets.
- Later, the term asteroid was used to describe these objects.
- In 2006, Ceres was classified as both an asteroid and a dwarf planet.

Giuseppe
Piazzi

Over the next few years, astronomers found other large bodies in the same region as Ceres, including Juno and Vesta. Most scientists then began referring to these objects as asteroids. By the late 1800's, astronomers had discovered hundreds of asteroids.

What Is the Connection Between Jupiter and the Main Belt?

Asteroids in the Main Belt with the planet Jupiter in the background, in an artist's illustration.

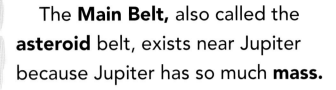

Highlights

- The Main Belt lies near Jupiter because of Jupiter's large mass.
- Jupiter's gravity keeps the asteroids in the outer part of the belt from drifting away.
- Scientists think that as the solar system formed, Jupiter's mass kept the material in the Main Belt from forming into a planet.

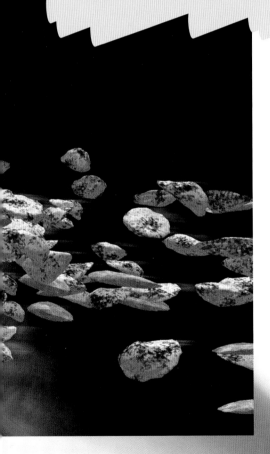

The **Main Belt,** also called the **asteroid** belt, exists near Jupiter because Jupiter has so much **mass.**

In the late 1700's, **astronomers** expected to find a **planet** in the area between the **orbits** of Jupiter and Mars. At that time, the orbits of all the known planets in the **solar system** followed a mathematical pattern. (Later discoveries, such as Neptune and the **dwarf planet** Pluto, would break that pattern, somewhat.) Instead of finding a planet between Jupiter and Mars, however, astronomers began to find asteroids.

Asteroids are made of the same material that formed the planets. Most scientists now think that the rocky matter in the Main Belt might eventually have become a planet. But the tremendous gravitational pull of Jupiter probably prevented these pieces from coming together to form a full-sized planet. Jupiter's **gravity** now keeps many of the asteroids in the outer Main Belt from wandering out of the area.

What Do Asteroids Look Like?

Asteroids have different kinds of surfaces. Some are dark. Others are very bright because they reflect much of the light that shines on them from the sun. The way asteroids look has a lot to do with the materials they are made of.

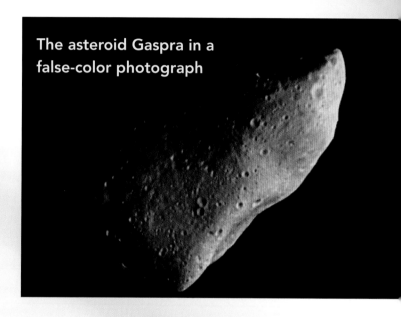

The asteroid Gaspra in a false-color photograph

Fun Fact

One of the most oddly shaped asteroids is named Kleopatra. Kleopatra has two rounded knobs joined by a slender center, making it look like a dog bone!

For example, dark asteroids are often made of substances rich in carbon. Brighter asteroids contain metal-rich **minerals** that reflect the sun's light. This shiny surface makes them more visible to scientists studying asteroids.

Some asteroids even have "mountains" on them. One

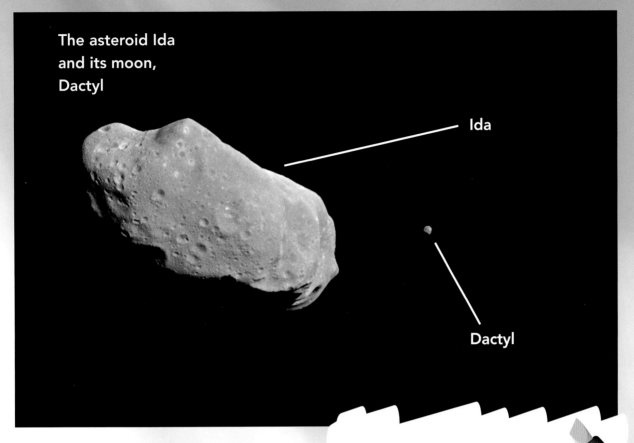

The asteroid Ida and its moon, Dactyl

Ida

Dactyl

such asteroid is named Vesta. In 1996, the Hubble Space Telescope took a picture of Vesta that showed a huge impact **crater.** Scientists think that a large object struck Vesta, creating the crater. The impact caused so much heat that a "mountain peak" was formed in the center of the crater as *molten* (melted) material flowed back into the crater.

Highlights

- The surfaces of asteroids differ, based on what the asteroids are made of.
- Asteroids that contain carbon are dark, while asteroids that contain minerals reflect the sun and appear brighter.
- Some asteroids have such features as craters.

Which Space Missions Have Studied Asteroids?

Before 1991, the only way scientists could study **asteroids** was by using telescopes from Earth. Since then, several space missions have sent **probes** to study asteroids in the **solar system.**

In 1991, the NASA space probe Galileo took the first close-up pictures of an asteroid, Gaspra. Galileo went on to study the asteroid Ida in 1993 and discovered its **moon,** Dactyl.

Highlights

- The first probe to study an asteroid was NASA's Galileo; Galileo photographed Gaspra and studied Ida.
- NEAR (later NEAR-Shoemaker) traveled to Mathilda and Eros.
- Dawn was launched in 2007 to study Vesta and Ceres.

In 1997, NASA's Near-Earth Asteroid Rendezvous (*RAHN duh voo*), or NEAR, probe studied the asteroid Mathilda and found many deep impact **craters.** In February 2000, the NEAR probe made history by going into **orbit** around the asteroid 433 Eros. That same year, the probe was renamed NEAR-Shoemaker, in honor of American astronomer Eugene Shoemaker (1928-1997). In 2001, NEAR-Shoemaker, reached the surface of Eros, taking a final picture as it landed.

In 2007, NASA launched the spacecraft Dawn to study the asteroids Vesta and Ceres.

An artist's drawing of the NEAR-Shoemaker probe as it approaches Eros

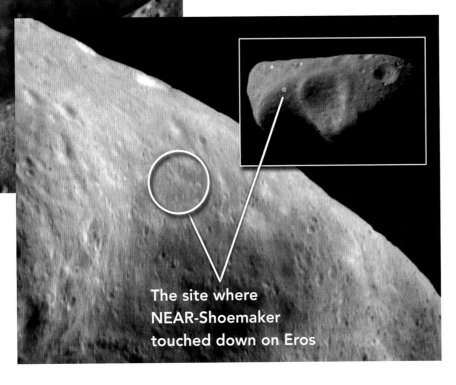

The site where NEAR-Shoemaker touched down on Eros

Two images of Eros taken by the NEAR-Shoemaker probe

What Can We Learn from Asteroids?

Scientists have learned quite a bit about the history of our **solar system** by studying **asteroids.** And most of what we know about asteroids comes from studying **meteorites.**

Meteorites are masses of stone or metal that have reached Earth from outer space without burning up. Most scientists agree that the majority of meteorites are fragments that have broken off from asteroids.

Asteroids are very interesting to scientists. Asteroids are very old, and most of them have not changed in billions of years. For these reasons, asteroids can tell scientists a great deal about the early solar system. For example, by looking at what asteroids are made of, scientists can learn what types of materials were common when the solar system was first beginning to form.

Highlights

- Many asteroids are billions of years old and may be left over from the formation of the solar system.
- Scientists study asteroids to learn about the early solar system.
- They learn about asteroids by examining meteorites that reach Earth; meteorites are usually pieces of matter that have splintered off from asteroids.

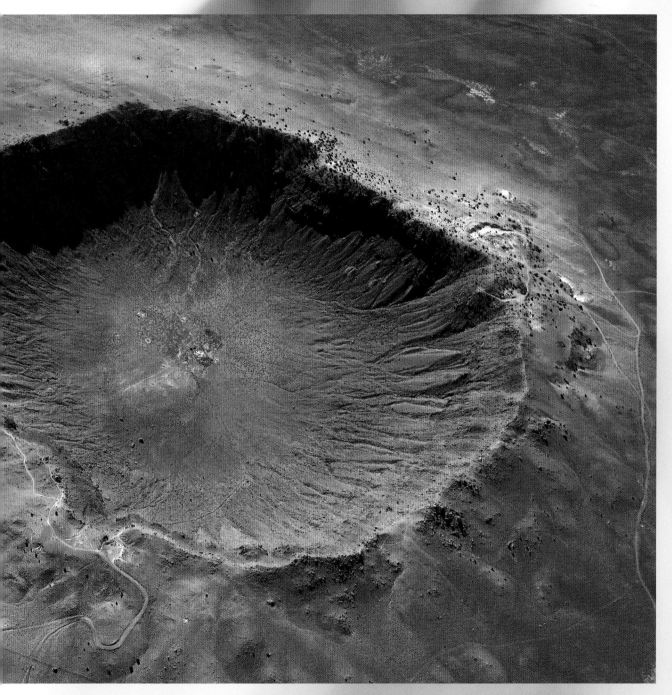

Barringer Meteor Crater, in Arizona, was formed when a meteorite struck Earth.

Are Asteroids Dangerous?

Asteroids are not usually dangerous. However, it is possible that a large asteroid could change its **orbit** around the sun and strike Earth. This has happened before in Earth's history. In fact, scientists think that an asteroid struck Earth about 65 million years ago. The impact may have caused such destruction to Earth's environment that it contributed to the extinction of the dinosaurs.

In 1989, an asteroid called 1989 FC—later named Asclepius—came very close to Earth. Many scientists became convinced that they should begin to track asteroids that orbit near Earth. In 1995, NASA began its Near-Earth Asteroid Tracking program. The scientists in this program look for asteroids that could collide with Earth and watch them to see if they are a danger to Earth. Scientists are even discussing plans of what to do if such an asteroid were on a course to strike Earth.

An imagined collision between an asteroid and Earth, in an artist's drawing

Highlights

- Most asteroids do not come close to striking Earth; however, the dinosaurs may have disappeared from Earth because of the effects of an asteroid that struck the planet about 65 million years ago.

- NASA scientists have been tracking near-Earth asteroids since 1995.

Jupiter and the Asteroids **59**

Glossary

ammonia A compound made up of nitrogen and hydrogen.

asteroid A small body made of rock, carbon, or metal that orbits the sun.

astronomer A scientist who studies stars, planets, and other objects in space.

atmosphere The mass of gases that surrounds a planet.

atom One of the basic units of matter. Atoms are more than a million times smaller than the thickness of a human hair.

comet A small body made of dirt and ice that orbits the sun.

convection current Movement or circulation that happens—for instance, in a planet's atmosphere— when warm gases rise and cooler gases sink.

core The center part of the inside of a planet.

crater A bowl-shaped depression on the surface of a moon or planet created by meteorite impact.

day The time it takes a planet to *rotate* (spin) once around its axis and come back to the same position in relation to the sun.

density The amount of matter in a given space.

diameter The distance of a straight line through the middle of a circle or anything shaped like a ball.

dwarf planet A round body in space that orbits a star but does not have enough gravitational pull to clear other objects from its orbit.

element A chemical element is any substance that contains only one kind of atom.

equator An imaginary circle around the middle of a planet.

fly-by Flight whereby a spacecraft flies near an object in space but does not land on or orbit that object.

gas giant Any of four planets— Jupiter, Saturn, Uranus, and Neptune—made up mostly of gas and liquid.

gravity The effect of a force of attraction that acts between all objects because of their mass (that is, the amount of matter they have).

helium The second most abundant and second lightest chemical element in the universe.

hydrogen The most abundant and the lightest chemical element in the universe.

magnetic field The space around a magnet or magnetized object where its magnetism can be detected.

Main Belt The region between Jupiter and Mars where most asteroids exist.

mass The amount of matter an object contains.

meteorite A mass of stone or metal from outer space that has reached the surface of a planet without burning up in that planet's atmosphere.

meteoroid A small object in space, believed to be the remains of a disintegrated comet or asteroid.

mineral An *inorganic* (nonliving) substance made up of crystals.

moon A smaller body that orbits a planet.

orbit The path that a smaller body takes around a larger body; for instance, the path that a planet takes around the sun. Also, to travel in an orbit.

planet A large, round body in space that orbits a star. A planet must have sufficient gravitational pull to clear other objects from the area of its orbit.

probe An unpiloted device sent to explore space. Most probes send *data* (information) from space.

satellite A natural object that orbits a planet or asteroid.

solar system A group of bodies in space made up of a star and the planets and other objects orbiting around that star.

water ice A term scientists use to describe frozen water, to distinguish it from ice that forms from other chemical substances.

year The time it takes a planet to complete one orbit around the sun.

For More Information

Books

Jupiter:

Destination Jupiter by Giles Sparrow (PowerKids Press, 2010)

Jupiter by George Capaccio (Marshall Cavendish Benchmark, 2010)

Max Goes to Jupiter by Jeffrey Bennett and others (Big Kid Science, 2009)

Asteroids:

Asteroids, Meteorites, and Comets by Josepha Sherman (Marshall Cavendish Benchmark, 2010)

Destination Asteroids, Comets, and Meteors by Giles Sparrow (PowerKids Press, 2010)

Web sites

Jupiter:

NASA's Solar System Exploration: Jupiter
http://sse.jpl.nasa.gov/planets/profile.cfm?Object=Jupiter&Display=Kids

National Geographic's Science and Space: Jupiter
http://science.nationalgeographic.com/science/space/solar-system/jupiter-article.html

Asteroids:

NASA's Solar System Exploration: Asteroids
http://sse.jpl.nasa.gov/planets/profile.cfm?Object=Asteroids&Display=Kids

National Geographic's Science and Space: Asteroids and Comets
http://science.nationalgeographic.com/science/space/solar-system/asteroids-comets-article.html

Index